SHUT UP AND TALK

An Effective Guide to Communication Skills

Thank you for purchasing my book!

To help you start putting what you will learn into practice, I'd like to offer you a **FREE Self Hypnosis Session** to build your **Confidence for Public Speaking!**

You can listen to the MP3 right here:

http://authorbillcalhoun.com/suatwelcome

Acknowledgments

This book is the culmination of a long-held vision.

It would be impossible to list all the special people who have supported this project over the years. I would, however, like to thank the following individuals who've been there along the way and supported me as I brought the vision to life.

First, thanks go to Barbara Smith, my "literary Yoda."

Second, my sincerest gratitude to Kate, my heaven-sent soul-supporter.

And finally, I want to thank the people and great land of Asia—and Singapore particularly—for enabling me to conceptualize and practice what I've written within these covers.

Bill C.

Shut Up And Talk: An Effective Guide to Communication Skills
©2013 Bill Calhoun

Self published edition 2013

All rights reserved. This book may not be reproduced in whole or in part, or transmitted in any form, or by any means electronic, mechanical, photocopying, recording, or other, without written permission from the author, except by a reviewer who may quote brief passages in a review.

Editor: Rebekah McGrady
Cover design and art: E-source; e-sourcemedia.com
Interior illustrations and design: Rebekah McGrady

ISBN 978-981-07-7037-2

Printed by CreateSpace

SHUT UP AND TALK

An Effective Guide to Communication Skills

BY
BILL CALHOUN

Contents

Introduction

The Value of Good Communication i

Inspiration...iv

How to Use This Book v

Chapter 1:

Foundations of Good Communication 1

Be a Leader 2

Make a Connection 5

Show Your Inner Self 11

Be Interesting! 13

Choose Your Words Carefully 16

Keep it Simple 20

Be a Good Listener 22

Stay Positive 25

Use Silence to Your Advantage.................. 28

Use Humor Well 30

Chapter 2:
Best Practices for
Business Communication 33

How to Introduce People 34

Tips for Good Teaching 37

Do's and Don't's of Talking to People in Authority 41

Do's and Don't's of Talking to Subordinates .. 43

How to Make an Effective Business Proposal 45

How to Apply for a Job 48

How to Present a Business Report 51

Make Your Ideas Count! 53

Best Ways to Give Constructive Criticism ... 56

How to Manage Interruptions 59

Chapter Three:
Become a Powerful Public Speaker 62

Your Body In Speaking 64

Your Voice in Speaking 68

How to Give an Informative Talk 71

Do's and Don't's of Using Visual Aids 76

How to Give a Speech for Any Occasion 80

How to Present and Receive Awards 83

Chapter 4:
How to Shine in
Social Communications 89

How to Be a Good Conversationalist 90

How to Give Compliments 95

Best Ways to Talk to People from Other Cultures 98

How to Apologize 100

Chapter Five:
Ideas for Additional Study 104

How to Improve Your Speaking Through Imitation 105

Best Ways to Improve Your Vocabulary 109

How to Use a Personal Slogan 111

How to Use Questions to Influence Others .. 114

How to Prove a Point Using Inductive Logic... 117

How to Prove a Point Using Deductive Logic ... 119

Afterword 124

Introduction

The Value of Good Communication

In my line of work I come across talented, amazing people every day. These are men and women who have great ideas and abilities to share—with their communities, their families, and the world.

If you're reading this book, you probably have an ambition to rise from your present position to something higher. You realize that reaching your goals depends largely on what you say, and how you say it.

Maybe you've learned English as a second language and want to refine your skills. Perhaps you already know the basics but need help using them in specific situations. Maybe you want to become more at ease in public speaking or in social settings, regardless of what language you speak.

If this sounds like you, keep reading.

I wrote this book for you and others like you—people who are talented and have a lot to offer, but who want to reach farther and higher. You could be a young person just starting out in life or a high-level corporate executive. No matter who you are, this book can help.

In today's busy and interconnected world, many of us are called upon to communicate in ways our parents and grandparents never imagined. We "talk" to people via electronic communication and often never meet them face to face. Many of us speak second languages and are required to converse with people from around the world. We are busier than ever. Yet it's never been more important to get our messages across clearly.

I know all this because I'm a living example. As an American making my home and career abroad, I understand the joys and challenges of communicating in our complex world.

I've developed and worked on a broad range of projects, from teaching dance to creating fitness programs and producing shows. In doing so, I've had the good fortune to work with amazing people to bring all this about. But it's never been primarily about the work. My success in these areas depends on my ability to communicate—with all kinds of people, in all situations. Without this skill, I could not have accomplished so much.

As I continue on this path, it's never been clearer to me how much we all need universal tools for good communication—tools that reach across cultural and language differences and help us connect at the level we all have in common—that of being human.

It's not always enough to be proficient in our native language. It's not always enough to speak another language reasonably well. People also need basic communication skills that will serve us well in the business world, in our personal lives, in public speaking, and social situations.

And so, my goal for this book is to give you those tools. Drawing on classic texts and the experience of countless examples from history, this book distills simple ideas that men and women have used to their benefit for centuries. Most of these ideas are aimed at helping you speak better, but they'll also help you with written communication—so important in our world today when we depend on machines to stay connected.

This is guidance you can trust.

Whoever you are—young or old, college-trained or self-educated, man or woman—you **can** improve your communication skills. In doing so, you can achieve more personal power, career success, and happiness.

You may or may not be a good natural speaker, but everyone who uses language is a speaker. You have real power in communicating at your command already. If you study and practice the simple lessons in these pages, you cannot fail to become a far more powerful, interesting, and effective communicator than you have ever been before.

Inspiration

I've taken my inspiration for this book from many places, including my own experience and those of men and women I greatly admire.

All together, these principles form a comprehensive reference about what it takes to communicate well and naturally in our complex modern world.

How to Use This Book

The book is organized into chapters that can be read in any order. Open it anywhere and you'll find simple ideas you can use today.

However, I encourage you to start with Chapter One. This chapter gives you basic rules for good communication that you can apply to any situation. Spend some time with these. Study and practice them and trust that over time they'll become natural parts of your thinking pattern. These ideas will give you a solid foundation in the basic and timeless skills of good communication.

Chapters Two, Three and Four go into detail about how to speak or write for specific settings. Chapter Two deals with business communication, Chapter Three is about public speaking, and Chapter Four will help you speak well and at ease in social settings.

Chapter Five includes ideas for additional study.

Within each chapter you will find short, easy-to-read lessons. These can be read in any order, and are meant to be studied one at a time. At the end of each lesson you'll find one or two exercises to help you put into practice what you've learned.

These lessons are meant to be applied to a broad range of situations. Don't limit yourself to the sorts of examples used in the text—be creative and you'll be amazed at how many ways you can use these ideas.

For example, you'll see reference over and over to the concept of making a connection with others. This idea is fundamental, because in its simplest form communication happens between people. Understanding the importance of making a connection can help you write a great email, develop a winning marketing campaign, or present a memorable speech before a packed auditorium.

You might find it helpful to use a notebook as you read through the lessons. Write down questions you want to investigate or points that speak to you directly. Every time you write something down, you reinforce your learning of that material.

My hope is for you to begin seeing quick results from your work with the book. Then, as you continue to study the lessons over time, you'll find the ideas are becoming a working part of your mind, supporting you no matter where life takes you.

Let's get started!

Bill C.

Chapter 1
Foundations of Good Communication

No matter where you're from or what you do for a living, chances are you have communication challenges.

It's only natural. In our hyper-connected world, we are called on to communicate with others in ways most of us never dreamed of even twenty years ago. We depend on electronic devices to keep us in touch with associates and loved ones. We may have ongoing and important business relationships with people all over the world. We may need to write to or talk with people from different cultural backgrounds or who speak languages we have not mastered.

And at the same time, the people we work with every day seem busier and busier. Where once we used to work set hours, people now routinely work at home or on the weekends. The line between business and social relationships seems to get fuzzier and fuzzier. Cell phones and other portable means of communicating mean we are always available to people—even when we might not want to be.

With all this going on, it's more important than ever to be skilled in some basic principles of communication for any situation.

Lucky for us, there are ideas to help us that people have relied on for centuries. For example, choosing the right words is just as important in writing an email as it is in giving a speech before a packed auditorium. Making eye contact helps you speak to your child as well as it does when interviewing job applicants.

If you read nothing else in this book, study the suggestions in this chapter and look for ways to put them into practice. Chances are you'll find all kinds of opportunities to benefit from them in your professional and personal life.

Be a Leader

One of the keys to being a good communicator in all situations is to adopt an attitude of leadership. If you can learn to "read" individuals and groups of people and guide communications proactively, you will go a long way towards being someone whose words and opinions are respected.

The key to being a leader in conversation and public speaking is simple -- but not necessarily easy: **make sure everything you say is worth listening to.**

A certain businessman seems to master every conversation he participates in, without appearing to dominate or take charge. He speaks directly to the point. He tells stories that illustrate concepts. He responds to other people's ideas, amplifying and illustrating them. He contributes new thoughts or ideas into the conversation.

This man projects a sense of great personal power. As a result, he has achieved many successes in his personal and professional life.

You can learn from his example. Take the lead in introducing topics of conversation. If you know who you're going to be speaking with, and in what situations, prepare ahead of time by thinking of topics that will be interesting to them.

At the same time, be careful about expressing your opinion. People are quick to recognize wise points of view, and the smart leader will refrain from offering an opinion too soon.

Listen instead. Gather evidence, reflect upon it, and then, when you're ready, you will speak with quiet authority.

It may seem obvious, but the best communicators have useful things to say. Stay current on issues and ideas. Read contemporary newspapers, magazines, and books. Try to be reasonably well-versed in a wide range of subjects so you'll never be at a loss for topics of conversation. If you have a deep well of knowledge at your command, you'll be able to make any conversation interesting and engaging.

At certain times, especially in business, you'll need to be able to control a speaking situation. For instance, you must lead when you're running a meeting or making a business presentation. Demonstrate at the beginning that you are taking a leadership role, and carry it through the entire time.

Don't allow the conversation to close until you're ready. When you've expressed everything you need to say, be the one to end the meeting with a statement that clearly shows it's finished.

In doing this, it's not necessary to be forceful or

manipulative. If you can lead in conversation graciously and with humility, and respect others' opinions, you will soon find yourself more confident and authoritative in your speaking. You'll relax and enjoy being with others more. You'll discover that conversation comes more easily and naturally, even with people who once may have seemed unapproachable.

So think about ways you can exercise leadership in your personal and professional interactions with others. Remember that communication happens between people. In all cases, be a participant—not a single voice. Value your own words and those of others, and you will attract respect.

Exercise. In your next group conversation, notice which person takes the lead. What techniques are being used? What is the effect?

Make a Connection

One of the keys to effective speaking in any situation is to connect with the people you're speaking to— whether this is in  a large public setting, or a one-on-one conversation.

This connection is crucial to understanding between humans—without it, all interchange of ideas and thoughts falls short. In fact, much of the skill of communication in business or personal life is nothing more than the conscious use of making connections with others. Some people are better at this than others by nature, but anyone can learn basic techniques and improve a great deal with practice.

Two ways to begin are to make eye contact and to establish common ground. Let's look at them one at a time.

Animal trainers know that to control the animals they're training, it's crucial to keep their eyes on them and maintain visual contact. People going into situations where the communication is likely to be unfriendly—or even hostile—know that by looking directly into the eyes of the people most likely to give them trouble, a human contact can be established and some of the tension can be relieved.

Eye contact connects two people, regardless of age, social status, country of origin, or language. You can have nothing in common with someone—including a language—and still make a strong connection.

A steady, direct look communicates authority and confidence. It also shows other people that you're interested in them and what they're saying. By paying people this compliment, they're comfortable being around you, and also more likely to remember what **you're** saying.

Practice making direct eye contact with others. A direct look concentrates your focus and makes you a good listener. Your memory is improved and you become more accurate in your perceptions and judgments. It also helps you perceive other people's points of view and sense the other person's emotional state.

The direct look also works in public speaking. Whether you're speaking to a large crowd or a small audience, look people in the face. If you allow yourself to become distracted too long with notes or your speech, or if you fix your attention on some vague point outside the eye contact of individual people, you lose your connection with the audience.

Instead, look around the room and make eye contact with as many people as possible—not just one or two. Let your personality meet theirs. Look from right to left to center—all around the room. The more people you connect with visually, the more people will be interested in your words and remember them.

Speak eye to eye, and heart to heart—not just once in a while, but always. Not just with your close friends, but with everyone you come into contact with. It will help in making you an excellent communicator and leader.

Next, let's look at how to establish a point of contact with words.

This point of contact is really nothing more than common ground. It's something that you and other people are both interested in—a shared value, story, or experience.

If you look for it, there's always some definite point of contact that can be established, even with strangers or people who appear unfriendly or challenging. The key is to know your audience and think about what you might have in common.

A business manager found herself with strangers on three different occasions all in one week. Within a few minutes time of meeting each one, she found some point of contact. One had been born within a few minutes drive of her own home town. Another had two sons attending the same school as her children. And the third had vacationed at the same resort she used to visit.

In each case the business manager felt immediately at ease and was therefore in a better position to speak effectively with all three people. The key was asking questions and getting to know people in order to establish a point of contact.

The common ground between old friends is what makes friendly conversations so delightful and enjoyable. Even a suggestion from a friend is more convincing than the most carefully thought-out argument of a stranger.

Here are some ideas for making a point of contact with someone:

- The memory of a shared experience
- People you know in common—mutual friends or acquaintances
- Similar educational background
- Common business interests
- A hobby that you both share
- Recent books or movies
- Can you think of others?

In public speaking as well as with individuals, it's just as important to have a point of contact. Try to show your audience you're on some common ground in life or work—that you, in effect, are one of them.

Appeal to your shared membership in a company, organization, or even your country. Refer to your shared experience of a recent local event.

Take some time to study the style of excellent public speakers. Notice how well they establish common ground. From that moment on, they cease to be strangers to their audience and become, to some degree, a friend or associate.

Exercise. During the course of a day, notice the eyes of people you talk to. Notice those who seem to be good speakers or communicators. What are they doing with their eyes?

Exercise. Think of three different people you're going to be meeting with soon. What points of contact can you make with each one?

Show Your Inner Self

A corollary to making points of contact with others is to be transparent with your whole self in your speaking. In addition to speaking honestly, this means letting your facial expression show your emotions.

People respond well to speakers who show their humanity and emotions through facial expressions and gestures. In historic times, a "radiant countenance" was often associated with great inner wisdom or power—even with genius. After all, speaking is a sort of telegraph between souls. The face is another means of sending the message. It brings personalities together.

An old man stands every day on a crowded street in New York City and sells a cheap mechanical device. As he demonstrates, he talks. His face lights up, becomes serious, changes all the while that he's explaining his product. He looks at individuals with kindness and humanity. People around him feel he's explaining a natural wonder of the world instead of a cheap throw-away product. Consciously or unconsciously, he's using his experience of being human—shown through facial expression—as part of his demonstration. He is making a strong connection with his audience.

And so, as you speak, whether to one person or a thousand, let your face light up with the changing emotions of what you say. This kind of expression is contagious, and it helps carry your thoughts and ideas to hearers. It draws attention and therefore also makes what you say more interesting.

Conversely, when you listen, let your face reflect the changing emotions of what you hear. The speaker will see your recognition and sympathy, and a connection will be made.

People who communicate with their whole selves will succeed far more easily than those who hide their personalities under a real, or assumed, mask of withdrawal and reservation. Throughout history, some cultures have prided themselves on impassive expressions that give nothing away. Such cultures have lived in environments where this was beneficial or necessary to survival.

But our modern, interconnected world demands free and close connections between human beings. Your success in social and business life will be affected by how well you can show your humanity, personality and self in both words and expression when you speak. Harmony between words and expression will make you a memorable speaker.

Exercise. As you go about your daily business, notice people with whom you exchange only a few words—for instance, a stranger in an elevator or the clerk who delivers your mail. Pay attention to their facial expressions. Which people make the impression of being better speakers?

Be Interesting!

Of course, to be effective at communication you will want to hold the interest of the people you're communicating with. This is harder than it seems, but some basic ideas can help anyone be interesting in any situation.

First, adapt yourself to your circumstances. Make a decision to be open to your surroundings and take cues from these and the people you're with. There's more than one way to be interesting, and what works with one person or group won't necessarily work with another.

A strong point of contact is the foundation for building interest. For example, the relationship between a parent and child is so close that the parent is keenly interested in whatever the child is doing. The child may say something silly or trivial, uninteresting to anyone but the parent. It's the warm relationship, or point of contact, that creates the interest.

In all interactions, even in the business world, remember that establishing a close point of contact will encourage interest between everyone involved.

Second, think about building curiosity. Human beings are innately curious, and you can use this fact to your advantage in your speaking.

A traveler to a Middle Eastern country heard a man speak in a country village. The man said,

"Ladies and gentlemen, I am a notorious swindler. I have come to swindle you. If you have any money in your pockets, go home. In fact, to prove what a swindler I am, listen to this."

And he took out a newspaper and read a story describing him as a dangerous swindler in a neighboring county.

Everyone in the crowd was fascinated. More people gathered around. The man's power of speaking held their attention, and he actually swindled the entire crowd just as he said he would. He had aroused interest because he appealed to the people's curiosity.

You don't have to swindle your friends and associates to hold their interest. Instead, when you're in conversation or speaking, say something unordinary. Or say something ordinary in an unusual way. Avoid the commonplace, and make use of humor and exaggeration if it's appropriate. Use distinctive or unusual gestures. Use visual aids, looking beyond what other people might commonly use and trying something new.

Engage with others as you speak. Remember that communication happens between people. Say something unusual, then wait and let others respond before you go forward. Become involved. Take interest in what others are saying, and you will also be seen as interesting.

All of these ideas will help you hold people's attention, and improve your communication in any setting.

Exercise. Think of one or two of the most interesting speakers you've ever heard. How did they gain interest?

Choose Your Words Carefully

It seems obvious that your effectiveness as a speaker depends largely on **what you say**—that is, on your choice of words.

At all times, you will want to say what you mean and mean what you say. The nearer you can get to this ideal in all your interactions, the better your communication will be and the more people will respect you.

To do this, you'll need to know what you mean, and then to choose the right words to express is. Even if this skill doesn't come naturally to you, you can strengthen it through practice. These guidelines will help.

Use definite words. Words can either be generic or specific. A generic word refers to a group or category—for instance, "animal." A specific word refers to a particular member of a group or category—for example, "Bengal tiger."

Although generic words communicate a lot, they don't call up a definite picture. Specific words suggest a definite, precise visual image or picture—you can see it in your mind. Using specific words whenever you can will make your speaking more powerful and interesting. That's because your listeners will "see" what you're saying as well as hearing it.

In the following examples, notice how much more interesting the second phrase is.

> *She showed me some souvenirs.*
> *She showed me some silver Balinese earrings.*
>
> *I went out on the water.*
> *I went out on a mountain lake.*
>
> *He made a long journey.*
> *He traveled a thousand kilometers.*

In general, follow the rule: be specific. You'll soon gain a reputation of being an interesting speaker.

Avoid slang. Avoid all slang except when you want to use it specifically to make a point. The occasional use of slang to make an impact is not a problem, but a habit of using slang weakens communication overall. Why?

Because slang words usually take the place of solid words with clear and maybe subtle shades of meaning.

Choose simple words. Avoid words that are overly long or complicated. Using too many bookish-sounding words can make you sound out of touch with regular people. It's possible and effective to communicate sophisticated ideas even with simple, clear language.

Avoid jargon. Jargon is technical language that's specific to a business or field. Chances are your own field of work or business has some language all its own that might not be understandable to people outside that area. If you must use jargon with people who might not know it, immediately explain what you mean.

Pay attention to correct usage. In every language there are certain words that people commonly misuse or mix up. If you had the good fortune to grow up around adults with good speech, you probably don't make many of these mistakes. Even if your usage isn't perfect, though, there are ways to cultivate an ear for it.

Just as artists learn from studying masters of the past, you too can improve your speech by listening to and reading masters of language. Study the speech of the best educated people, including those who may no longer be living. Read classic literature to infuse the sound of correct usage into your mind. Listen to tapes or watch movies of high quality to develop an ear for good usage.

You might even buy a small pocket dictionary to keep with you in case you encounter a word you don't know how to pronounce. This is especially useful when you find such words in writing.

Cultivate a habit of speaking slowly and carefully. Try to pronounce each syllable and not slur them together. These practices will help you avoid mispronouncing words.

Practice these techniques regularly, and you'll have a better chance of being understood the first time. After all, understanding between people is the heart of good communication.

Exercise. Develop a habit of observing your own speaking. Do you tend to repeat certain favorite words or phrases too often? How much do you use slang or jargon?

Exercise. Think of someone you consider an excellent communicator. Now think about how fast that person speaks, and consider what you can learn from this.

Exercise. Next time you're having a casual conversation, try describing an experience using specific language.

Keep it Simple

Some of the great novelists of English literature wrote about characters who spoke with something called "total recall." People with total recall tend to talk forever, giving all related details, and taking a long time to arrive at a conclusion.

Some people find it almost impossible to speak directly to a point. You meet such people, not only in the pages of literature, but in everyday life. Everybody knows someone like this. Or maybe you are someone like this.

But great leaders in business, politics, and all arenas usually speak simply and to the point. People with great levels of responsibility don't have time or the inclination for petty details or roundabout expressions. They know what they want to say, and they say it.

If you want to be a good communicator, you will want to practice speaking briefly and directly. This may require you to spend some time thinking about what you really want to say. Learn to listen to your own thoughts or use a journal to help you sort them out.

Of course, bouncing ideas off another person is a powerful way to think things through and develop ideas. This sort of interaction is an important way human beings help each other. But be careful to do this at appropriate times. Some people use roundabout conversation in professional situations as a way to arrive at what they really think or believe. Modern life is so complex, so full of demands on everyone's time, that people have little patience for others who aren't sure of what they want to say.

Take some regular time for solitude. Do your thinking ahead of time, and you'll avoid the need to use other people for this purpose.

Another element of keeping things simple is to avoid non-essential details. Especially, keep the conversation focused on the subject at hand—do your best not to let it veer away to a slightly related subject. Be polite yet firm in following your own line of thought clearly and quickly to a definite conclusion. Then, and only then, turn your attention to some other topic.

Exercise. You're talking with someone over a business lunch about something important. The other person has the habit of turning the subject away to trivial matters without knowing it. How can you keep the conversation on track?

Be a Good Listener

One of the most important keys to good communication is not speaking at all.

The person who monopolizes the conversation and doesn't allow others to speak is not a good communicator. It seems obvious that communication is a pattern of speaking and listening. But the listening part can be harder to master than it seems.

If you speak all or most of the time, you're actually at a disadvantage in conversation. That's because you haven't allowed yourself to hear how the other person is responding. You won't know for sure what effect you're having, and you could unknowingly say something that will not help you in the long run.

In the classic "Sherlock Holmes" stories, author Conan

Doyle cleverly makes the famous detective a good listener. His assistant, Watson, is less effective. Watson is always interrupting, or ready to act before having all the necessary information. Sherlock Holmes, on the other hand, asks quick questions, listens, and gives others the freedom to express themselves fully.

You can learn some techniques that will help you be a better listener—and therefore a better communicator.

In every social or business conversation, listen while your friends or coworkers express themselves. Give them the space to talk, as a fisherman gives a fish space to swim on the hook while at the same time keeping hold of the line.

Acknowledge that you hear others with nods and gestures. From time to time, restrict your own speech to almost nothing and see what happens.

Another kind of "listening" is intuition, or learning to sense other people's thoughts, feelings or responses.

Imagine if you had the ability to see fully into the minds of other people. How would this change the way you speak and communicate? Chances are, you'd never feel unprepared or at a loss for words.

No one can ever fully have this ability, of course, but at some level we do see into other people's minds because

we are generally motivated by the same things.

All people, in any situation or condition, have many of the same desires and fears. This is true across all ages and cultures. Knowing this, you can trust that the way you'd respond to a given situation is likely to be shared by others.

Don't assume that you're in the other person's place. Assume that you actually **are** the other person. Although we don't often recognize this, most people are naturally gifted with understanding human nature because we ourselves are human. To the extent that we understand ourselves, we can also understand others.

Here's an example of how this intuition can work in a business setting. If you have something to sell, imagine what kind of speech would induce you to buy a product. Use what you know in making your own sales pitches. On the contrary, think of what kind of communication would turn you away from buying, and avoid that kind of pitch.

Forget yourself, and try to understand the influences that might be affecting the other people you're speaking with. Are they in poor health? Is their business in bad shape, or have they recently suffered the death of a loved one? You'll find such understanding goes a long way toward good communication with others.

Cultivating intuition and giving others the space to express themselves are the keys to listening—which in turn is central to good communication. Although these skills seem outwardly passive, they actually put you in a position of strength, influence and authentic connection to others.

Practice listening for a while and you'll likely be amazed at the results in your relationships.

Exercise. You're making a sales call to an individual you don't know well. How will it help you sell your product if you give the other person time to speak freely?

Exercise. One of your employees makes a lot of errors that cost your company money. You don't want to fire him, but you must confront the situation. What kind of words will help you and your employee the most?

Stay Positive

Our world is full of negative messages in the media. Cynicism runs rampant in many modes of public and private communication.

To be certain, negativity can attract short-term interest. In the long run, though, people who give off a sense of quiet optimism or even neutrality will gain the most respect as communicators. One of the greatest ways to cultivate power as a speaker is to continue to be good-natured in spite of almost every temptation to give in to anger, argument, or cynicism.

There are times and occasions when anger may be so justified that you must express it. You feel that if you don't express yourself, you are being less than honest or authentic. Certainly, events happen for which measured outrage may be the only appropriate response. In general, though, these situations happen infrequently. Not many occurrences are truly life or death situations. So reserve your anger for times when it's truly justified.

Speaking angrily or complaining about trivial things actually places the speaker in a weak position rather than a strong one. Giving in to angry emotions also causes people to lose focus and possibly the ability to make sound judgments. In contrast, maintaining a good nature gives the speaker a great deal of personal power.

An employee became offended at the way his supervisor was treating him. One day when the supervisor pointed out a mistake, the employee burst into angry, abusive language. Letting loose with frustration that had been building for months, he called his supervisor a series of names.

How did the supervisor react? He proved his right to a

superior position. By remaining calm and good-natured, he was able to recognize the employee's value to the company. He did not strike out or fire the employee. Had he joined the employee in reactive anger, the company might have lost a valuable worker and the two might have become seriously estranged. By staying cool, the supervisor maintained a position of strength.

The key to maintaining good nature in the face of negativity is this: as far as possible, respond to such situations rather than reacting. Choose to hold on to a positive or neutral attitude and approach. Take the time to think through a rational response rather than letting your emotions take over.

It takes time and practice to master the skill of remaining positive, but the rewards are huge.

Exercise. You frequently have lunch with a friend who often talks about mutual acquaintances with contempt. How would it work to your disadvantage to join in this? How does it work to your advantage to avoid this kind of conversation?

Exercise. You find, in your daily life, that many things go wrong—you have many real problems. Most people complain about such conditions. How does complaining affect those people? Does it help?

Use Silence to Your Advantage

Some of the world's most powerful men and women have been people of few words, even silence. These are individuals who have communed with their own souls and have lived, so to speak, in a great silence. And yet they have done and said great things, and influenced the world for good.

Look around you today at the men and women you associate with. You will probably see many who talk and chatter mindlessly, without saying much that's important and sometimes being so careless that other people are harmed.

Shakespeare had this kind of person in mind when he wrote, in "The Merchant of Venice," that

"Gratiano speaks an infinite deal of nothing, more than any man in all Venice."

No one admires this kind of speech, and typically such people are not admired either. They might be funny or good to have at a party, but individuals given to this kind of communication are seldom leaders.

On the other hand, chances are you have a few friends or coworkers who are considered more thoughtful and respected. They are probably people who think before they speak. This is true even if such people are naturally outgoing and conversational. Their opinions are worth knowing and when they do speak, they do so carefully and at appropriate times.

Cultivating silence does not mean you must become introverted if you have an extroverted personality. It means to build some silence into your life and choosing your words carefully when you do speak. Consider these ideas:

- Don't waste energy on idle, shallow talk. When you speak, have something useful to say.
- Don't feel you must speak just to fill up a silence. Let a silent moment sit.
- Use silence for reflection and good judgment.

Exercise. Whether you are outgoing or reserved, how can you incorporate periods of silence into your life?

Use Humor Well

The ability to use wit and humor well will add tremendously to your conversation and public speaking, and will bring delight and enjoyment to everyone.

Someone has said that if a person has the gift of humor and uses it well, that individual can make a fortune. The nineteenth century American writer, Mark Twain, is still one of the best examples of this.

Certainly, people who use humor well will attract friends. And a public speaker who does so will attract audiences.

But what are the appropriate uses of humor?

It helps to consider that humor is often best used as a means of relief from suffering—of which there is always plenty in the world. People who are suffering from any kind of hardship, whether physical, emotional, mental, or financial, often fall back on humor to get a larger perspective. And who in the world does not have some sort of personal or public hardship?

It's said that "laughter is the best medicine," and it's true that appropriate humor can lift the lowest spirit.

But humor can also be used to damage and tear down. Too much "comedy" is expressed at the expense of others, in the form of ridicule or criticism. While this type of humor may offer temporary enjoyment, at a deeper level it only adds to the overall suffering of human beings.

Consider these ideas for using humor well.

- Develop the habit of smiling when you speak.
- Look for humor in everyday situations, even grim ones.
- Practice telling a story well, emphasizing humorous aspects.

Above all, avoid profanity and off-color remarks, or those who ridicule individuals or groups of people. This kind of humor is so common that you may wonder how you can be funny without it. But people who use it aren't necessarily respected for their opinions on serious or substantial matters. It's definitely possible to find deeply gratifying humor without resorting to remarks that degrade others.

When in doubt, laugh at yourself.

Exercise. Why do great plays and pieces of literature that are considered tragic often have elements of comedy?

Chapter 2
Best Practices for Business Communication

Business communications have changed drastically, even in our lifetimes.

Just a few decades ago, the electric typewriter was cutting edge technology in the office. Telephones stayed on top of people's desks and in their homes. People wrote paper letters and mailed them through the post.

It was a far cry from the world we live in now, where so much of the world's business happens electronically.

It might seem that the rules for good business communication also need to be rewritten. To be sure, there are some special considerations for making the most of electronic communication technology.

At the same time, the main factor in business communication hasn't changed, and that is: people. No matter how technologically advanced we become, we will never grow out of being human. And the foundation of communication isn't technology. It's humanity.

The ideas in Chapter Two are very relevant to today's workplace and business environment. In fact, they might even be more important than ever because of the new challenging situations we have for communicating in the world of information technology. We don't always see our associates face to face, so we can't rely on body language or facial expressions to interpret meaning. Sometimes we're forced to put our communications in short, size-limited messages online.

Technology moves faster than we do, and it's easy to forget the human element. In such a world, returning to basic principles of good interaction with others can bring in a humanizing touch, whether we're talking in person, or text messaging, etc. And that's an idea that never gets old.

How to Introduce People

How often have you been introduced to a person you've never met, and afterward could not remember the person's name?

The purpose of introductions is to make two strangers acquainted. It is to get to know a new person. But what does this really mean?

To know people means much more than to know their names. It usually means to know what they do, and what sort of people they are.

What, then, is an effective way to introduce people? A good introduction has at least three parts: name, a distinguishing feature, and what your relationship to the person is. Think about sharing enough information so that you convey to others the knowledge you already have of the people you're introducing.

First, speak names very clearly, enunciating every syllable. Say the names a little louder than your ordinary speech.

Next, say something distinctive about the person you're introducing. In business settings this usually involves saying what the person does for employment. For instance,

> *"This is Rachel Liu. She's chief counsel at Aegis Auto Company."*
> *"I'd like to introduce David Lee, City Editor of the Middletown Daily News."*

Third, establish a point of contact. That is, say how you know the person or what your connection is. This will help your friends remember the name. For example:

> *"We were childhood friends and classmates."*
> *"One of the most creative people I have ever met."*

When you yourself are introduced, look into the eyes of the person you just met. Shake hands, and repeat his or her name, trying to imprint the name and face in your mind. If you don't hear a name clearly, or if you find that you've forgotten it almost immediately after hearing it, ask for it again and repeat it. It shows interest in the other person to keep with this until you have the name fixed.

If the person introducing you has given you a point of contact, follow up on this. Use it to begin a brief conversation. If no point of contact has been made, use a question to find one.

> *"You and Mary are old friends?"*
> *"You are also in the car business?"*

At no point during an introduction should you appear rushed or hurried. The opportunity to make new friends or associates is precious. Take your time.

Exercise. You've gone to lunch with a young friend just out of college and looking for career advice. At the cafe, you run into the president of your company. Practice introducing them to each other.

Tips for Good Teaching

As you progress in life and your career, it's very likely that you will be called on to teach at some point. This could be as simple as teaching a group of employees how to use an office machine or as complex as instructing an auditorium full of people in a scientific theory.

There is a proven method you can use to help you and the people you're teaching, no matter what the subject is. The heart of this method is to start with the known and move ahead to the unknown.

Create interest in your subject. Show the practical value of what you're going to be teaching. Tell your audience what good it is, and how it can be used to benefit people, or a business, or health, etc.

Make a strong point of contact with what the audience already knows. That is, find a foundation to build on. Your students or audience will almost certainly have some pre-existing knowledge of the subject matter you're sharing, and it will put everyone at ease to use this as a stepping stone to the new material.

For example, if you were teaching chemistry to people who had never studied it formally before, you could start with what they already know about how chemistry works in everyday life, using examples from common household objects. There's virtually no subject that doesn't have some point of contact in ordinary, everyday experience.

Your success as a teacher depends on finding points of contact—not just one point, but many—not just once, but throughout the course of your teaching. This is one of the most important secrets of good teaching.

Make every step clear. You want to teach in such a way that the least knowledgeable students can understand if they pay attention. This will save you from two teaching pitfalls: teaching over the heads of your students, and going too quickly.

Teach in a spiral system. Basically, this means to come back again and again to points you have already covered, but adding something new each time you return. This system can be tricky to plan out, but if you master it you'll be much more effective as a teacher. Your students have many small opportunities to "test" what they're learning, and ask questions, as you circle back to it again and again. Repetition enforces learning.

Have a plan. Everyone's busy, and it's tempting to go into a teaching environment and simply begin speaking from your own knowledge. Resist this temptation and teach from a pre-organized plan or outline.

Summarize. At the end of every teaching session, summarize what you've covered and emphasize the main points that students should have picked up.

Compliment students. Give positive reinforcement to your students for the progress they've made. Even a horse appreciates a friendly pat of the hand now and then. Acknowledge that your students are trying hard and progressing, especially if the subject matter is especially difficult. Be as patient as possible with slow learners, and never criticize.

If you go into a teaching situation expecting students to be slow and make mistakes, you can focus on how you'll handle these situations rather than letting them frustrate you.

Teach principles, methods, processes, and concepts. As much as you can, teach principles and concepts that students can apply as they take the new material into their lives. Details are often less important, but can be used to illustrate overall concepts and ideas. Remind students to take these principles and apply them as often as possible, because it's true that ***practice makes perfect.***

Exercise. You've been asked to teach a seminar on a field in which you're an expert. You have three hours and an audience of 500. What will you cover, and how will you present it?

Do's and Don't's of Talking to People in Authority

Have you ever worked with people who constantly complain that they could run an organization better than the bosses? People who have lots of great ideas and complain when others don't implement them?

Think about it. Where are those people today, and did they ever rise to a position of leadership?

Imagine you're called into a meeting with your immediate supervisor. You have talent, ability, and skill...and he knows it. That's why you're paid to do your job.

How will you speak with him?

Are you nervous or flustered? Falling over yourself to give compliments, trying to make him happy?

Are you resentful? Are you uninterested or distracted?

Although they are your superiors, you have more power than you know. All of these attitudes can teach your superiors to treat you in ways that will make you feel even worse.

How you behave around them directly influences how they treat you.

The key to successfully relating to people in positions of authority is to preserve your self-respect while also respecting their authority.

It's all right to be ambitious, but respect that you are not yet in the position that your superiors are.

Don't try to flatter them. Be pleasant, interested, and honorable.

As in all communications, it will help to find a point of contact on which you are equals. Maybe you share a love of a certain sport or have recently read the same book. No matter how much authority your superiors might have over you on the organizational chart, as human beings you are equal. This is true even if you have the bad luck to have a supervisor who behaves as if you are not, in fact, equal.

Remain firm in your self-respect. Show respect for the positions of those above you. Respect them as humans, and you will have cordial relationships with your superiors.

Exercise. You are introduced to an elected official of significant authority, and you have a few minutes for conversation. Think out a few ideas for what you might say.

Do's and Don't's of Talking to Subordinates

A young woman had a small account in a New York bank. One day a bank official, who knew the woman's bank account was small, spoke to the young woman in a condescending way.
> *"But I have an account here,"* the young woman protested.
> *"Your account is too small to interest us!"* snapped the bank official.

The woman withdrew her small account.

Several days later, business at the bank was upset by a withdrawal of several million dollars. It became known that the young woman with the small account had also controlled the large account.

This story illustrates the first rule of speaking with people who may be subordinate or inferior in any way, whether position, wealth, or educational level:

It never pays to be condescending or overbearing.

One day the manager of a large corporation harshly criticized one of the subordinates. The criticism mounted until the manager was throwing personal insults toward the other man. The subordinate was helpless and the manager gloated that he had been powerful enough to get away with this behavior.

Within six months the manager had been fired. The younger, subordinate man had friends that the manager didn't know about.

Never use your authority as a simple display of power.

There are appropriate ways to offer constructive criticism and suggestions—described in this chapter—but relying on sheer power is not the way to do it.

The best military leaders are those who gain the devotion and respect of the soldiers in their command. Very often this happens because the leaders are attentive to the needs of each soldier, no matter how low he is in rank.

Show attention to subordinates and treat them as individuals.

In conclusion, remember the fable of the lion and the mouse. A mouse angered a sleeping lion but begged the huge cat not to harm him. The lion released the mouse, and later, when the lion was netted by hunters, the mouse saved the lion by gnawing through the ropes.

Be courteous and respectful toward subordinates.

Exercise. One of the people you supervise has been neglecting his work. Think out a way to bring up the subject and discuss it in a way that's helpful to everyone.

How to Make an Effective Business Proposal

No matter what your field of employment, there will almost certainly be times when you need to make a proposal of some sort. Asking for a job interview is one example. Selling a product is another, and making a proposal for a service is another. In each case, you're asking someone to listen while you "sell" an idea, product, or service.

How will you make the most of your time and maximize your chance of success?

A key idea, and one that's often overlooked, is to commit to yourself that every proposal you make will benefit the person or people you're proposing it to. This value is based on honesty and integrity, and will have long-reaching rewards for you if you're patient. You might even memorize this statement:

> *"Every proposal I make will somehow be helpful or useful to others."*

If you have this commitment clearly in mind, you can meet the other person with a spirit of confidence and goodwill.

To prepare for your appointment, anticipate and identify a problem (or problems) the other person has that only you or your proposal can solve. Your next job is to make the need felt. Up until now, the person or company is carrying on well enough without your assistance. Do enough research to find out particulars about the organization, to prepare you to make your case. You might say something like,

> *"Mr. Assad, my name is Sally Frye of Blue Sky Marketing Company. We will guarantee to produce a marketing campaign for you that will bring a return of at least 3000 responses a month."*

Here, you've made an inducement based on a need you've identified Mr. Assad has. You've also promised something you think will help him. And, because of your commitment to being helpful, you have promised something you believe you can really deliver.

Another approach to this step is to demonstrate how other people or groups are using your solution, and what benefits they're enjoying. You might show examples of campaigns that you feel will benefit Mr. Assad's company, and then follow up with a specific proposal tailor-made for him.

The same outline can work for requesting a raise or a promotion. Propose how you can solve a problem or meet a need, show what you have done before, and then make your request.

A specific communication technique that will help you in making proposals is to maintain a leadership role in the meeting. While always being respectful and courteous, direct the meeting with quiet authority. In this way, you will demonstrate your own self-respect, which invites the respect of others. You will also ensure that all your points are communicated clearly.

Be quick to accept new suggestions, and be certain to avoid all contradiction or opposition. Allow the person you're speaking with plenty of time for thought and questions, but be sure that you hold on to the leadership role in the conversation.

Exercise. Develop the steps of a meeting in which you propose a series of articles for a national publication.

How to Apply for a Job

You know how uncomfortable it can be to apply for a position or face an interview with a room full of people. You know the feeling of nervousness and the importance of making a good impression. You also know how discouraging it is not to be successful.

What is the best approach for a successful job application or interview? Are there skills that can be learned? The answer may be approached by looking at tactics that don't work.

First, think about the volumes of guidance available to the modern job-seeker. This ranges from detailed instructions on how to dress all the way to specific answers to give in response to interview questions. One is advised to treat oneself as a sort of commodity that can be sold or advertised.

There are merits to this approach, but there are also limitations. Remember the basic rules of selling a proposal to someone, outlined in the previous lesson. These can be applied with good results to the process of applying for a job.

At every step of your process, speak with an eye toward being sincerely useful and honest.

Avoid too many questions focused on what the organization could offer you, such as:

> *Do you have job openings?*
> *How much do you pay?*
> *What are the hours and fringe benefits?*

If you need to ask questions like this, bring them up at the end after you have focused on what you can bring the organization.

Share honestly and completely what you have done and what you can do, such as:

> *I was the comptroller at Stern and Davis, which has just gone out of business.*
> *I have just completed my undergraduate degree in economics.*
> *Alex Chang, for whom I was a draftsman, suggested that I apply here for a drafting position.*

Begin with your most important information. There are two ways to go wrong with this part of the interview. One is to overstate your abilities or misrepresent them to the interviewer.

If you can't actually promise to increase the company's revenue by 25% in the next three years, you should not say that you can. If your best quality isn't really working too hard, you should not say that it is. If you use pre-conceived answers that don't actually resonate with you, you may talk yourself into a job you really aren't prepared for.

The other way to go wrong in sharing what you can do is to be embarrassed and not say enough. In fear of being boastful, some people underestimate their abilities or simply wait for the interviewer to ask questions.

The solution in both situations is to give all the facts. It's not necessary to be arrogant or make claims you think will impress. In fact, you'll garner more respect if you state the truth in simple but factual terms. You will also know you've spoken with integrity.

Exercise. Think about what you might say in applying for a position exactly like the one you now have.

How to Present a Business Report

Almost every day, people give some kind of report to others—even if it's just a short answer to a question about your job. Often you will be required to give a substantial report, either oral or written, on some project or body of work.

Following a few simple steps will ensure your report is thorough and that you present yourself in the best possible light. These steps can be used as a template for very brief reports or summaries, or longer, more formal presentations. What they have in common is that you're reporting to someone else on work you've done independently, or a project you've been asked to complete.

Think about these four steps in preparing and presenting any oral or written report.

Define the reason for the report. This shows that you understood what was asked of you and reminds the person who asked, in case he or she has forgotten. For example,

> *"You asked me yesterday to find out which of our marketing projects are getting the best returns."*

Summarize what you found briefly. If possible, keep it to one simple and clear sentence, such as:

> *"I found that the campaign called 'The Boy' has brought better returns than any of the others."*

Give supporting details after the summary to illustrate what you've said. For example:

> *"Looking over our third quarter data, 'The Woman' brought in 172 returns; 'The Man' brought in 129, and 'The Boy' brought in 462. The money returns were......,"* etc.

Make a recommendation based on your work or observations. Something like:

> "I recommend that you hire the Global Publicity Company to create another campaign like 'The Boy.'"

A thorough report will include all of these steps. Of course, for reports on very complex projects or those involving lots of data, Steps Three and Four will incorporate more explanation and supporting information. Try to keep Steps One and Two brief no matter what. Busy executives will appreciate your efforts to save them time by summarizing very briefly why you're presenting the report and what you found.

Exercise. Your professional association has asked you for a report on plans for an upcoming membership campaign. Draft the report following the four steps above.

Make Your Ideas Count!

The work of the world thrives on new ideas. Whether you work for yourself or for a large organization or somewhere in between, invariably you'll have opportunities to offer your ideas and suggestions to others. These may be employers, or clients, business partners, or anyone else in your network. And wise managers and employers will listen.

For example, let's say you're an employee in a medium-sized office. As you go about your daily work you notice ways the business could be improved—saving time, money, or maybe both. You'd like to share your ideas with your supervisors, but you don't  want to waste their time. You want them to listen to you and have the best chance of acting on your ideas.

How will you do this?

First, make sure your idea is a good one.

Is it realistic? Can it actually be put into practice? Would it interfere with your own job or those of your co-workers? To explore this, you might want to bounce the idea off a detached person—maybe a personal friend or family member who has nothing at stake in your job.

Often people who offer suggestions don't consider all sides of the situation. They have vague ideas rather than well-thought-out solutions. By merely presenting an idea with no plan for execution, you might actually be giving your boss another problem to think about. Imagine how much more she or he would appreciate your idea if you also provide a plan for executing it.

Therefore, only offer good ideas that you know can be put into practice.

It helps to clarify your idea on paper. This will help you organize your thoughts and examine all sides. Once you've decided it's practical, try to summarize it in one coherent sentence. At the same time, think of two or three clear arguments that show the problem your idea will solve—in other words, identify a need.

Second, having done all this preparation, find a good time to share your idea with the relevant people. Make sure you approach them when they're able to give you their full attention without distraction.

Third, simply state your case. Start with the need you've identified, and then briefly state your idea. Describe how it could be put into action. It's probably best to do this in person, verbally, but there may be times when you need to write it out in a formal memo or other written format.

And finally, having done all this, stop.

If you've spoken simply and clearly, there's no need to say more.

If you chose a good time to present your idea, the other people heard it. Even if they don't act on your suggestion, chances are excellent that you made a good impression and they'll listen again to your ideas in the future.

Exercise. Think of a suggestion that might help the organization you work for, or some other group you belong to. Sketch out a verbal presentation of your idea, using two or three sentences to outline the need first, and then one sentence for the solution.

Best Ways to Give Constructive Criticism

It takes a subtle and skilled communicator to correct someone else's mistakes or give correction without personal criticism.

Consider how many meanings the word *criticize* can imply.

"He criticized me."

"She read a critique."
"He is a movie critic."

The first sentence implies "He found fault with me,"' while the second means that "She read an analysis of something" and the third refers to someone who reviews movies.

The word "critic" really means nothing more than an expert, or someone who can see something wrong and correct it. Most adults have to give criticism of some sort every day—that is, to correct situations that need adjustment. Whether it's with children, employees, or with themselves, the mature individual cultivates this ability.

The key is knowing the difference between helpful, constructive correction, and **fault-finding.**

If your communication with others (or even yourself) consists of nothing but fault-finding, you will do little more than irritate and demoralize. Fault-finding focuses on the negative, or what is being done wrong. Constructive criticism—that is, constructive correction—focuses on the positive; in other words, a better way to do things.

Imagine you own a restaurant and have hired a new cook. On her first day, you see her going about the work in a way that wastes time and ingredients.

Correct the situation by showing her another way to do it, not merely by pointing out what she's doing wrong.

Maybe she doesn't know a better way. Say something like,

> *"It will go faster if you do this, and you won't waste the lettuce."*

Your administrative assistant has a habit of coming in half an hour late, day after day. Instead of saying, "You've been late nine times in the last two weeks. Don't let it happen again," remind him "I need you here at eight o'clock sharp, every day."

Another principle of constructive criticism is to point out improvement or progress. Tell your new cook that her work last week was excellent and quick. Thank your assistant for arriving on time every day and remind him that it's important to you.

Finally, constructive criticism should never focus on the person, but always on the action. It's appropriate and necessary for superiors and people in authority to make corrections in the work of people under them. But it's never appropriate to criticize their character or dignity.

These ideas can work for constructive criticism in social relationships as well as business settings. Make a commitment to staying focused on the positive and not finding fault, and all your relationships will be smoother.

Exercise. One of your helpers is doing substandard work. Think out some positive, constructive criticism that will help her and benefit you.

How to Manage Interruptions

Interruptions are a fact of modern business life, but they can seriously disrupt the flow of communication needed to get work done effectively.

No doubt you've had an experience like the following more times than you'd like to remember.

For a long time you've needed to meet with a supervisor to report on an important project. You finally have your meeting, and you sit down to present your report.

Almost at once, your manager gets a phone call. You wait while he finishes, and begin again. Soon another employee bursts in with important papers for the manager to sign. You continue, and there's another phone call. Finally, before you have a chance to get to your main point, your manager stands and announces that he must dash to another meeting. You've wasted your time and accomplished nothing.

Interruptions will always be a fact of life, but there are some practical ways to minimize them.

First, think ahead and try to schedule your appointment when your manager is least likely to be interrupted. Maybe he comes in early or works late just to have blocks of uninterrupted time. Offer to meet him during one of these periods.

Second, accept that interruptions will happen, and anticipate them. Make up your mind that you will be interrupted. Think through in advance what you want to say, and make sure you say the most important things in the first sentence or two of your meeting. Go on with details until the first interruption. When it comes, at least you will have expressed your key points.

Third, be the one to renew the conversation. It's human nature not to remember what was happening before unplanned interruptions, so take the lead in bringing your manager's attention back to what you were saying. Repeat the last few words you said before he was interrupted, avoiding at all times any hint of frustration or hurry. Simply start the conversation again as if nothing had happened.

Interruptions in modern life are so frequent that it's easy to feel one's time is controlled by them. These tips will help you regain a sense of at least some control and ability to communicate even in face of these distractions.

Exercise. You're about to go for a job interview. Anticipate that the employer will be interrupted, and plan out how you will respond to this situation.

Chapter Three
Become a Powerful Public Speaker

As long as human beings live and work together, there will be a need for good public speakers. This has been true for thousands of years. And this need will probably only grow as the world becomes more interconnected.

What an amazing skill it is to be able to speak well to other people and influence them for good. The modern man or woman who really wants to make an impact can make use of a few basic principles for public speaking. These ideas have given ordinary people power to influence and reach countless others throughout history.

To begin training as a good public speaker, it's a good idea to study and really get some mastery over the communication skills outlined in Chapter One. For review, those skills are:

- Be a Leader
- Make A Connection
- Show Your Inner Self
- Be Interesting!
- Choose Your Words Carefully
- Keep It Simple
- Be a Good Listener
- Stay Positive
- Use Silence to Your Advantage
- Use Humor Wisely

At first glance, it might seem you wouldn't need good listening skills for public speaking. But in fact this tactic is very relevant. It helps immensely if you can "listen" intuitively to the audience to judge what impact your speech is having, and to note any nonverbal communication that people may be sending.

In similar ways, the other fundamental communication skills in Chapter One will help you in all your public speaking. Study and practice them first. Then move ahead with the techniques in this chapter.

Your Body In Speaking

The way you present yourself physically in public speaking is almost as important as what you say. That's because all eyes will be on you: you're making a visual impression as well as a verbal one.

Although it's visual, this impression doesn't rest primarily on your bodily appearance. Whether you're tall or short, young or old, these factors are less important to your visual communication than your posture and gestures. What you do with your body, however, can speak volumes.

The main thing to keep in mind is to be as natural as possible. Almost everyone is nervous about public speaking, but it's worth practicing holding yourself in an easy, relaxed posture.

At the same time, you want to project an attitude of dignity and respect. If your natural manner is to slouch and shove your hands in your pockets, you'll want to cultivate a more refined posture. It's amazing what effect an authoritative, yet natural, manner can have on an audience, even before you've started to speak.

Whenever possible, you should stand up when you speak before an audience. This is true even in a relatively small setting like a business meeting. When you stand, you breathe more deeply and hold your shoulders straighter. You feel more authoritative and others will be more inclined to pay attention.

Stand tall, with your weight generally distributed evenly between your feet. You might want to have one foot slightly in front of the other. Keep your shoulders back and head high. Try not to lean against anything. Move around somewhat as you would if you were alone, neither slouching nor standing stiffly. You may need to practice this posture in front of a mirror to get comfortable with it.

Of course, there may be situations in which it's better to bend these rules, especially in an informal setting. You might want to stay seated, depending on the arrangement of the room you're in. You might need to adopt a very casual demeanor if you're speaking in a very informal environment. But in general, maintain a sense of dignity, subtle authority, and naturalness, and whatever you say will have more impact.

Another important part of your physical presence is what you do with your hands. Like the voice, hands and other parts of the body are powerful tools of expression.

Because it's so common to be nervous when speaking publicly—especially for the first time—many people deal with their anxiety by doing something distracting with the hands. They jam them in their pockets or clench the side of a table or podium. They nervously toy with their clothing, tap a pencil, or shuffle papers.

There's a story about a boy who could only recite in class when he twisted the button on his shirt. He failed miserably when his sister cut off the button.

The problem with nervous hand gestures is that they cause a sense of anxiety among listeners, so that no one is relaxed. Consciously or unconsciously, the audience will take its cues from you. If you're nervous, it will also put them in a state of tension. Nervous actions with the hands will also cause the hearers to focus attention on **those actions** rather than what you're saying.

And so, as far as possible, try not to fall into any habitual pattern with your hands.

This doesn't mean your hands should be idle. You can use them very effectively to emphasize your thoughts. Let them rise now and then into natural gestures as they would if you were in a casual, social setting.

Most people do this, to some extent, without thinking. Think about the impact of a fist slammed on a podium to drive home a point, or the visual aid of counting on the fingers, or gesturing toward a particular member of the audience to ask a question. The communication in each instance is a combination of words and bodily expression.

Some people, of course, use their hands to excess when speaking. You may have heard the story of the two gesticulating Italians who fell off a boat. Neither could swim, yet they stayed afloat until they were rescued.

> *"But you said you couldn't swim!" said one of their rescuers.*
>
> *"We couldn't," was the answer. "We just kept talking."*

There's a happy medium to be found between over-gesturing and not using the hands at all.

You can also use your whole body to help you through the content of your speech. For instance, when you change subjects or begin a new section of your speech, shift your position slightly or face a different part of the audience. The shift in bodily position will indicate to the audience that you're also shifting thoughts, and help them follow your logic.

The key to using gestures well is to find a balance. Gestures of the hands and body should be used to emphasize points, but never to overshadow them. And the best way to do this is to be natural, trusting both your words and your natural physical expressions.

Exercise. Have an imaginary conversation with someone in front of a mirror. Letting your hands rest easily on your lap or by your sides, observe what they naturally do as you speak. Now try the same thing with your hands clasped tightly in front of you. Notice how different this feels!

Exercise. Imagine you're speaking to a visitor in your office. Get into a comfortable position for speaking, paying particular attention to the position of your hands.

Your Voice in Speaking

Once you've mastered some techniques for how you'll stand and use your body in public speaking, consider how you use your voice.

As noted above, a natural posture of the body communicates dignity and ease. It helps the audience and speaker both to relax and pay attention to what's being said. In much the same way, using an easy, natural speaking voice will help you get your message across.

Inexperienced public speakers often speak too quickly out of nervousness—or in a high-pitched voice, or too loudly. While these are common reactions to being in front of a crowd, the best public speakers have learned to overcome them.

The problem with speaking too quickly or in an unnatural tone of voice is that it can create a sense of anxiety among listeners, much as shuffling your hands nervously can create tension. Again, the result of nervous actions is that the audience pays attention to your anxiety rather than your message. In addition, if you speak too quickly, they might miss key points of your speech.

Although your heart may be racing and you may feel charged with nervous energy, you can use this energy as a source of strength. Instead of discharging it into the audience, think about holding some of your verbal power in reserve. There are several useful ways to go about this.

First, cultivate the habit of speaking in an easy, calm manner.

You want to keep your voice loud enough to reach the person or persons you want to hear you, **but no louder.**

If you're on a platform or stage above a large audience, the same rule applies. Whether or not you use a microphone, be sure everyone in the audience can hear you. But don't waste energy speaking any more loudly you need to.

The speaker who shouts will not impress an audience nearly as much as one who uses a voice that leaves the impression of power held in reserve.

Second, speak slowly.

Fast speaking is not effective in private or in public communication. People who speak too fast are almost certain to run their words together, leaving no time for emphasis. It's too easy for the hearer to mistake the real meaning.

So slow down. Hold power in reserve. By practicing control of your voice and body, you'll project an attitude of quiet authority and will enjoy a much more attentive audience.

Exercise. Read the following aloud, using an easy, calm, and slow voice.

> *The valley lay spread before him. Just beyond the foothills he saw the little village with its gray roofs and two or three steeples peeking among the trees. Beyond was the bright line of the river. Opposite rose the other side of the valley wall, a great wooded hill. North and south he saw cultivated fields stretching away into the distance. This was the countryside of his childhood.*

How to Give an Informative Talk

An informative talk, or lecture, is an extended speech on a single topic, usually for the purpose of teaching or instructing. Such talks can also be given for entertainment, and many are both educational and fun. Whatever the purpose, some key points will help you be effective and memorable as a speaker.

Overall, you want to remember to maintain a constant point of contact between your audience and your subject matter. In other words, continually point out to them why your material is relevant, through illustrations and examples.

You can accomplish this if you make sure to give definite, specific information, and if you do it in a way that the audience enjoys. Vague information presented in a dry and disconnected manner is not likely to hold the listeners' interest.

Here are some general guidelines for an informational or entertaining lecture.

Speak clearly and distinctly. It's essential to speak loudly enough so everyone can hear, but don't overdo it. Don't rush through or you will convey an attitude of nervousness.

Speak on one definite topic. When we sit down to listen to a speaker, we are essentially giving that person our trust for a given amount of time. Through our willingness to listen, we're saying,

> *"I'm giving up an hour of my valuable time, and I trust you to make it worthwhile."*

Wandering too far off-topic will quickly cause you to lose the trust of your audience. They will get frustrated and may even get up and leave. Follow a clear line of thought from the minute you start speaking until you close.

If you have to veer off the subject to illustrate a point, wait until at least a few minutes into your speech to do so. By then you will have gained the trust of your audience and they won't mind following you down your logical path. You might even acknowledge that you're veering and will come back, by saying something direct like,

"Now stay with me while we talk about X, but we'll come back to Y in just a minute."

In this way you guide your audience along on your train of thought, and reassure them that their trust in you is well-placed.

Speak briefly. A good rule of thumb is never to speak for more than an hour. Usually, it's best to be even shorter than that.

Make a connection. Immediately, when you start speaking, establish a point of contact between yourself and the audience. Often this takes the form of a joke, which eases the initial tension. Or you might say something that definitely makes them feel you're one of them.

When musical performers say what they remember about the last time they were in a town, they are establishing a point of contact between themselves and the audience.

Say what you're going to be speaking about right away. Think in terms of a "thesis statement" such as you might use in an essay. This will set the audience at ease and let them know what to expect. For instance,

> *"I'm going to speak tonight about astronomy. I'll be sharing some general information about the field, but my main purpose is to show you that astronomy is practical, fascinating, and enjoyable."*

You have now outlined what you're going to talk about, down to the three subsections of material you'll present. Having laid these out, your audience will trust you to follow this general outline. Make sure you do so.

Make another connection. Once you've established a point of contact between yourself and the audience, make another between **your audience** and the **subject matter.** This means telling them why the subject matter is important to them; why it's relevant and why they should care. Don't assume the people are already interested or know why the subject matter relates to them. By consciously pointing out reasons, they will pay more attention and find your talk more interesting. For example:

> *"You may think the study of stars has little to do with your life. But actually, we are all astronomers. We watch the sun rise and set, we look at the sky for weather. If we live by the ocean, we trust*

completely the predictions in the almanac about when the tide will come in." Etc.

Continue to make connections between the subject matter and audience throughout your talk.

Draw illustrations and examples from simple and familiar situations. This will make your talk much more interesting than if you refer to obscure examples or ideas that are specific to a certain field. For example:

> *"The surface of the moon is wrinkled like the skin of a dried-up apple. It's this way for the same reason the apple is, too—an interior that has shrunk."*

Show the practical side of your subject. Show your listeners how they can use your information right away in their lives or work. Give understandable, accessible examples and ideas for applying what you've shared.

By following these guidelines any time you're presenting information in a talk or lecture, you will establish yourself as an interesting speaker who will be heard and understood.

Exercise. Outline a talk on a subject that you excel in. What will be your main thesis, and how will you establish a contact between your audience and this subject?

Do's and Don't's of Using Visual Aids

Visual aids have always been an important way for speakers to emphasize and illustrate their presentations. On the surface, it seems that using illustrations will make the speaker's job easier. Yet it's actually harder to give a good illustration lecture or talk than one based strictly on speaking.

Why is this?

The answer is that the temptation is always there to let the illustrations take the leading role, rather than to support the spoken material. This is true whether you're holding up photographs to show people, or using sophisticated technology for visual aid.

It helps to understand the difference between an illustrated talk and an exhibition of pictures. Naturally, if your purpose is to present a slide show of photos you took on your vacation, your words will be used to support the photos—not the other way around. But if your main purpose is to present information, remember that you will be more effective if **you** present it, rather than expecting the illustrations to do that for you. Good communication comes from people, not objects.

Here are some common mistakes people make using visual aids in public speaking:

- Giving a disconnected talk, treating every illustration as a separate topic.
- Failing to speak on the subjects illustrated, thereby dividing the listeners' attention between words and pictures.
- Turning toward the illustrations, making it hard for listeners to hear.
- Using the illustrations as the focal point of the talk, rather than illustrating the focal point of the speech.
- Speaking too long.
- Standing in one position.

Here are some guidelines for making illustrations work for you and not distract from what you're saying.

Arrange the illustrations in the order they will need to appear to support your spoken outline.

Set up a quiet, unobtrusive way to switch between illustrations. If someone else is helping you, devise a quiet code or sign language to indicate that it's time to go to the next one.

Present your talk almost as if there were no illustrations. This can be hard to do, but try to avoid saying things like, "Here we have a picture of…."

Instead, speak on your subject, letting the illustrations support the words without calling special attention to them.

There are exceptions to this rule, of course. Say, for instance, you're giving a talk on the work of a given artist. In this case you'd definitely want to draw the audience's attention to each slide or photograph, pointing out the use of line, color, or form, etc. In such a case, the illustrations are the point of the talk, so it makes sense to say "Please turn your attention to this slide…., " etc.

Set up the illustrations to correspond directly with your talk. While you don't want to say, "This next picture shows....," you do want to speak on the very subject in the illustrations. If your words say one thing and the photos say another, it's like having two people speaking at the same time. The audience will be very confused.

Make the talk connected. Try to speak so there's no break between pictures, without pausing or delaying while they're changed. Remember that you are there to speak, not to exhibit pictures.

Speak directly to the audience. Avoid turning your back or your side to your hearers while you look at the illustrations. Look at them out of the corner of your eye, but face the audience at all times. Don't stand at the back of the room and operate the machinery changing the illustrations unless, as noted above, the focus of your talk really is the visuals.

Center your talk around one main idea. For example, "Greece is noted for its archaeological ruins," or "Spain is the land of romance." By clearly defining this idea for yourself and your audience, you will more easily use the illustrations to support it, rather than wandering.

Make your lecture develop in power. Hold your strongest points until near the close to build to a climax.

Be brief. Limit your talk to one hour at the longest—preferably shorter.

Speak clearly and loudly enough for everyone to hear. If you're speaking in the dark especially, you will probably need to speak more loudly than usual since you have no eye contact with the audience.

As you can see, there's more to giving a successful illustrated talk than one might imagine. In some ways this type of public speaking is more challenging than a straight verbal speech. However, using visual aids can be a powerful support to your message.

Keep these ideas in mind and your next illustrated talk is sure to be a good one.

Exercise. Plan an illustrated talk on a subject that you care about, remembering that your words are the focus of the talk, and the illustrations are there to support them.

How to Give a Speech for Any Occasion

Modern life holds many opportunities for public speaking. Anyone who is involved in his or her community, whether through clubs, religious organizations, professional associations, or other groups will likely be

called upon at some time to speak before others.

Here are some examples of times you may be asked to speak.

- An historical celebration in your community
- An anniversary
- A funeral
- Welcome to a distinguished visitor
- The opening of a new industry, facility, or place of commerce
- A school or family reunion
- The beginning of a sporting event
- The completion of a public work
- A retirement party

How would it help you if you had an outline you could use for creating a speech for any of these occasions? The following guidelines offer a good starting point.

First, describe the events leading up to the current occasion. You might say something like:

> *"Forty years ago a young man came to this city. He didn't have a job, and he didn't know anyone. But he had an idea and a dream—one that could help thousands of young people who just needed a little help." (Continue with an overview of the work you're about to praise.)*

Second, say the purpose of today's occasion.

> *"Today, we who have benefited so much from this man's vision and work have come together to recognize his contribution to our community."* Etc.

Third, put the occasion in a larger context—introduce timeless principles of some sort.

> *"We're here today not only to honor one man, but also to hold up the ideals he has believed in and worked toward for these forty years. With his unwavering commitment to young people in our town, he has reminded us that the future is with the young, and by supporting them, we support our shared humanity and experience."*

Fourth, use the larger context to inspire the people in the audience, to bring them in and make them part of it.

> *"Let's show this valued member of our town how much we appreciate his selfless work on behalf of our entire population by dedicating ourselves to following in his footsteps. Let's all of us ask ourselves -- in what small or large ways can we carry this vision forward?"*

Fifth, wrap up by returning to the opening statement about the occasion.

"By taking these ideas to heart, each of us can help ensure that our friend's last forty years of work will carry forward for the next forty years and beyond."

By following these general ideas and being sincere in your words, you can rise above the temporary events of the day or occasion, and place them in a larger picture that resonates with everyone. This approach will make your address inviting, relevant to the audience, and powerful.

Exercise. Think out the steps of a public address for the opening of a new library.

How to Present and Receive Awards

At some point in your professional or personal life it's very likely that you'll be called on to present an award to someone— or you'll receive one yourself. Maybe you will do both on many occasions. Let's look at some general ideas for how to present awards, followed by a gracious way to accept one.

A general rule for presenting an award is to speak from the general to the specific.

Let's say you're a judge at a competition of some sort, and have been chosen to present the final judges' decision. Follow this progression.

Make a contact with the audience by acknowledging your role.

> *"It has been a real pleasure for the other judges and me to help with this competition."*

Say something about the general value of the work that's been on display.

> *"Musical performance is a great field for artistic expression. It enriches the lives of those who perform and those who listen. We appreciate the efforts of all the musicians here today who have devoted their time and energy to a pursuit that benefits our society so deeply."*

Say something about the value of this competition.

> *"The competition tonight was unusually good. All the musicians showed a high degree of talent as well as creative expression in their choice of material....etc."*

Say something about the best work in the competition.

> *"One player in particular mastered every element that the judges were asked to consider in their selection of a winner."*

Make the award.

> *"Therefore the judges, while congratulating all the fine performers here tonight, award the prize to Miss Tan."*

To sum up, go from the general to the specific in making the award. Use whatever complimentary and non-offensive humor you want, if it's appropriate to the setting. Above all, wait until the very end to name the winner.

This technique is simple and logical, and will add dignity to the event and to you as a speaker.

Now let's consider what you'll say when the time comes for you to **receive** an award.

In general, it's much easier to present an award than to speak publicly to accept one. You should simultaneously speak without any conceit, and also be personal in what you say.

The best way to bring in the personal element is to speak with a sense of gratitude.

"I can't tell you how much I appreciate the award you've just presented to me. I can't think of any that has touched me more in many years. I recognize every person who was behind this decision, and all I can say is thank you, very sincerely."

Saying something like this shows the personal side of your personality. You practice transparency and let the hearers see a side of you that you might not often share. In this way you make a strong connection with the audience, and strengthen the bond you already have with the people who are making the award.

Next, acknowledge the cooperation of others as honestly as possible. Hardly anything worth noting happens without the support and encouragement of a network of people, and you will do well to name them and what they did. But be careful to be honest—don't fall into simple flattery.

> *"I cannot take full responsibility for the work that is being recognized today. It could not have happened without the full cooperation of ...." (go on to describe who supported, and what they did).*

Say something about the actual gift you've received.

> *"This beautiful memento will always remind me, not of the work I've done but of your loyalty, support, and friendship."*

Say something about your intentions for the future, and then express your thanks again.

> *"With your continued support I intend to extend this project even further....(say some specific plans if possible). Once again, my deepest thanks for this honor, and for your friendship."*

These outlines for giving and receiving awards will serve you in any occasion.

Exercise. You've helped coach a youth athletic team that has won a series of games. The team has given you a valuable gift of appreciation. Outline a brief but heartfelt acceptance statement.

Chapter 4
How to Shine in Social Communications

In this chapter you'll learn ideas that will guide you in speaking in private life and social settings. If you apply them, you'll not only make your conversations more effective, but they will also be more enjoyable for you and your friends.

Whatever your personality, most people can use help in performing better in social situations. Although these places are often where we go to relax and let the cares of the day fall away, it's in our best interest to pay attention to how we interact in these relationships. Being careless in social situations can harm others and ourselves.

Remember also that mastering speech in everyday life leads to greater skill in speaking in public and business affairs.

How to Be a Good Conversationalist

What makes good conversation? What makes a person pleasant and memorable to speak with, someone whose company you enjoy and whose conversation you remember?

Try this exercise. Think of someone you love talking to. Remember how it feels to be around her or him. Now, on a piece of paper, make a list of all the qualities you can think of in a good conversationalist—using your friend as a starting point.

Then write down opposite qualities after each word, for contrast. In this way you'll have a list of positive qualities and their opposites—something like this:

Quiet/Loud
Unassuming/Arrogant
Precise/Careless
Respectful/Crude
Honest/Deceitful
Sincere/Flattering
Understanding/Argumentative
Listens Well/Dominates
Stays on Point/Fragmented
Interesting/Dull
Humorous/Heavy
Friendly/Antagonistic
Complimentary/Sarcastic
Uplifting/Degrading

Now think about your own style of conversational speaking.

Be honest. Look over the list and check off any characteristic that applies to you, from either side of the list. Do you have a lot of "good" qualities? Excellent! Which characteristics from the "negative" side apply to you?

Think of ways you might gradually work on improving these points.

Maybe you tend to speak in a loud, overbearing way. Make a commitment to speak more softly and spend more time listening. Or maybe you rely too much on crude humor, thinking it acceptable to tell off-color jokes because people usually laugh at them. If so, try to come up with some ways you can still be funny without resorting to inappropriate remarks.

Are you sarcastic? Although sarcastic and satirical language are common in modern conversation and the media, these practices are based on negative thoughts rather than positive.

The Latin root for the word *sarcasm* means "to tear flesh" or "to bite the lip in rage." At its heart, sarcasm tears down; it does not build up. So think about what effect you want to have and what impression you want to leave before leaning too far on sarcasm.

Honest praise is a distinct feature of all conversation. Use it freely, but don't flatter—your praise must be sincere or you will be seen as a less than honest person.

Some people have a conversational habit of being argumentative, sometimes without even knowing it. They contradict or refute almost every comment made by others. If this is your style, try instead to yield and respect others' comments and points of view. If you feel very strongly compelled to disagree or offer a differing opinion, do so respectfully, by first acknowledging the merits of the other view before sharing your own.

If you want to be truly well-liked in social settings, make a firm commitment never to belittle anyone, even in jest. Other people might laugh at the time, but be sure they'll remember the remarks you make at their expense.

Try to say only things that are uplifting or useful in some way. Be bright, humorous, and interesting. It's fine to be clever and quick, but avoid anything that will lower anyone's standards of honor or respect. This sounds old-fashioned, but people will remember the good feeling you leave them with after a conversation in your company.

Being a good conversationalist is also important in the most intimate setting — that of your home. Taking care about how you speak to your family members communicates that you value them, and models good speaking behavior for children.

The home is also a place you can practice conversational skills that you'll take out into the larger world. Consider these questions.

- In your home, do you share what happened during your day with the people around you?
- Do you speak to the entire family, trying to find topics that are interesting to everyone?
- Do you repeat funny stories or anecdotes you've heard or read?
- Do you talk about the important news of the day?
- Do you read out loud to your children?
- Do you describe interesting or beautiful things you've seen or experienced?
- Do you suggest topics of conversation that make people think?
- Do you try to add to the conversations and topics that others bring up?
- Do you speak hopefully, with an optimistic outlook on life?

Your family members will be interested in your day's work or happenings. Tell them about these, but be interesting. Speak at a level that everyone will understand. Leave out unimportant details and share what's unusual or fascinating.

If you've heard a funny or uplifting story, tell it as if you were doing so in front of an audience. Try doing this every day, and you'll build up skill as a **raconteur**, or storyteller.

Lead the family in discussing important news of the day, being careful to avoid finding fault with world leaders or others in public life. Try to show that people in positions of power are doing the best they can, but that they, like everyone, are dealing with forces and events beyond their control. Speak hopefully and compassionately, and you will build your skill in speaking with wisdom and moderation to larger groups and in the outer world.

Make your conversation at home as bright and interesting as you can. Read aloud from the newspaper or a short story, making every effort to read clearly. Practice good grammar. Listen to your loved ones, and if they find fault with something you say, be grateful for the opportunity to learn from their honesty.

By practicing all these ideas at home, you can greatly develop your own capacity as an excellent speaker in the world at large.

Exercise. Look over the list at the opening of this lesson. Is there a particular practice you could improve? Set a goal of working on this quality in your home every day if possible. At the end of a month, re-evaluate yourself. What has improved? What have you learned?

How to Give Compliments

There's an old saying that you can catch more flies with honey than with vinegar. The meaning is clear. People respond better to compliments than they do to criticism—an obvious truth that is often not followed in daily conversation.

A man was so bothered by his wife's temper that he went to his lawyer to file for divorce.

"Why not help her change her temper?" asked the lawyer.

"Impossible!" said the man. "It can't be done."

"Compliment her," said the shrewd lawyer. "Surely there must be something she does or says that you still like. Tell the truth, but compliment her."

It was hard work at first, but the man gave it a try. He was surprised to find that, as he practiced complimenting his wife, he found more and more to compliment. And as he did, his wife found less and less to be angry about.

If used with moderation and reason, complimenting can be a very good communication tool. But if it's insincere, badly timed, or extravagant, it can do more damage than good.

Human beings seem never to outgrow their childlike love of praise. Most people know when they've done a good job, and like to be recognized. At the same time, people also know their shortcomings and limitations. It's usually easy to tell when someone is giving an insincere compliment or merely trying to flatter.

People naturally dislike **too many** compliments, and distrust the person who gives them. They realize the praise is forced and is probably meant to manipulate. It then stops being a compliment and becomes simply an insult.

Cultivate a habit of recognizing excellence in the people around you, and letting them know you see it. Be simple, sincere, and natural. Use simple phrases of acknowledgement like "Yes, that's right," or "I like your thinking," or "Your judgment is good."

In addition, nods, smiles, and other non-verbal gestures can communicate sincere approval. Look for ways to add these genuine expressions of praise into your daily speaking with others. They add grace and compassion to communication, and at the same time earn you respect as a speaker and individual.

Exercise. How do you feel when someone pays you a genuine compliment for a personality trait you appreciate in yourself, or a job you're proud of? Do you think others respond the same way to sincere praise?

Best Ways to Talk to People from Other Cultures

As with so many situations, the secret to good communications with people from other countries (or who may not speak your language) is to find a point of contact.

If you meet a foreigner on the street who needs directions or a simple question answered, you can get along well by using the simplest language possible. Speak slowly and clearly, and if needed, use diagrams or gestures to indicate directions. Your attitude of helpfulness is all the point of contact that's needed.

Suppose, however, that you meet someone from another country under a more complicated setting. You're at a social gathering and seated next to someone whose native language and cultural background appear very different from your own.

What topics will be of interest? How can you find common ground?

In general, a good place to start is by talking about the other person's country. You could ask about current events there, or great people and their achievements, or the natural setting and geography of that country. If you've traveled to the other person's land, by all means talk about that. You might also discuss the relations, past or present, between your country and the other person's.

This approach presupposes that you're generally aware of current events, history, and cultures in other places. If you have opportunity to speak or meet with people from other countries often, this is a wonderful reason to read widely and take an interest in issues and cultures outside your own.

Exercise. You're introduced to a distinguished visitor from Italy. Think about some topics you might suggest for conversation.

How to Apologize

Sooner or later—and probably sooner than later—everyone has to make apologies for something done or not done; a hurt caused another person or a failed commitment. But most people are not taught how to do this.

Think about the purpose of an apology.

You should have done something, and you didn't do it. Or you did something you should not have done. You may have very good reasons for this, including reasons that were totally beyond your control. In such cases it's human nature to blame—a situation, an external force, another person, the weather. Even so, blaming seldom has a good result.

What are your alternatives?

The answer may be found in this principle: put yourself in

the other person's position, and put him or her in yours. See the other side, and be willing to take responsibility for your part—even if you feel you were influenced by causes beyond your control. In doing so, you will certainly reduce the other person's desire to become defensive and attack you. While this might seem, on the surface, a position of weakness, it actually allows you to maintain a high degree of personal power and integrity.

Let's say you're a sales representative for a large corporation. You should have made an entry in the company record of sales, but you did not. The daily records are now off-balance. Someone higher up has complained, and you're called upon to explain the mistake.

Immediately take the questioner's part, and acknowledge what has happened.

> *"Ms Lambert, that entry was not made. I should have made it, and it's not acceptable that I failed to do so. If I were you I would be annoyed. The only reason I know of is that, just as I was about to make the entry, my phone rang and I answered it. Then I forgot to get back to what I had been doing previously. I don't blame you for being irritated."*

There is very little your manager can say in response. You've anticipated everything she might say, and said it for her. In doing so, you robbed her words of their force.

In other cases, someone may simply be unhappy with a legitimate choice you have made. For example, several employees under your direction are eligible for promotion. However, your organizational budget only allows you to promote two. What will you say to the employees who were not promoted? What if they take a position of resentment or blame toward you?

In such circumstances, an apology is not needed; however, you can still do your best to amend the situation.

Once again, try to take the other person's point of view. Acknowledge how much you value that employee, and that you would also be disappointed if your positions were exchanged. You might, very briefly, give your best reason for having made the decision you made. State that you place a high value on good relations with the other person and you hope they can continue.

To summarize, the best approach to making apologies or amending situations of disappointment is to be willing to put yourself in the other person's position. Acknowledge your part in the situation, including errors if you made them. Do all this openly and as honestly as you can, maintaining your own sense of self-respect.

Exercise. You agreed to meet a friend at four o'clock. You forgot the meeting. Think through what you will say to make amends to your friend.

Chapter Five
Ideas for Additional Study

You have now learned many principles of good communication. Starting with the fundamentals in Chapter One, you've studied techniques and concepts that can help you become a more effective speaker in business situations, in public speaking, and in your social life. All these areas, of course, overlap and influence each other.

The following are ideas for additional study that can help you refine and develop your skills even further. Read through them and see if they give you any ideas to use in your daily life.

For instance, the lesson on using a personal slogan is similar to the modern practice of personal branding. In fact, the idea of adopting a personal motto or phrase to associate with one's personality or business ethics is nothing new. You can use it to your advantage, and you may find new ways to apply it beyond those outlined here.

Even if you don't consciously apply the lessons in this chapter, it can be useful to read through them and let them work into your mind. You might be surprised to find yourself drawing on them when you least expect it.

How to Improve Your Speaking Through Imitation

It's hard to create something brand new, but it's easy to imitate what has already been done.

Throughout history, artists in all fields have learned by studying and copying the masters, eventually blending those influences with their own unique expressions. In a sense, all of civilization has been built this way, on the foundation of imitation.

One of the best ways to learn the art of good communication is to imitate good speakers. You can do this in many ways, including listening to them, and reading out loud. Let's look at each of these in turn.

There are innumerable chances to hear good language spoken, increasingly so as communications technology advances. Listen to eloquent, renowned speakers in person or in the media and let the sounds of the words and sentence structure soak into your mind. Notice which sounds and practices you like, and try to incorporate them into your own speaking.

While listening to good speech is very beneficial, your own speaking can deteriorate if you make a habit of listening to crude, unskilled speakers. In spite of their best intentions, human beings imitate each other in speech. Spend too much time around unskilled or poor speakers, and you will likely pick up some bad habits.

These ideas are especially important if you converse regularly in a second language. Maybe you travel abroad often for your employment and use one or more languages besides your native one. Try to spend time with good native speakers. Listen to recorded speeches or high quality media presentations in the languages you want to master.

Another way to improve your speech through imitation is to read excellent writing out loud. In a way, this gives you the opportunity to hear high-quality speech in your own voice.

Try this idea with your family. If you develop a habit of reading aloud every night, you will probably have several eager listeners.

Read short items of interest from a high quality newspaper or good magazines of general interest. If you try to read an entire book out loud you will probably have so many interruptions that everyone will end up frustrated. But even busy people can find time to read a short article or news item. Take advantage of small bits of time to do this. You can practice every technique you need for public and business speaking right inside your own home.

You want your audience to hear you. Therefore, practice modulating your voice to be loud enough, but not overpowering. You want your hearers to understand you completely, so practice speaking very clearly and slowly. You want your audience to be interested, so read with expression and eye contact if possible.

The effect of this practice day after day, week after week, will so improve your enunciation and general speaking ability that you will gain more than you could with weeks of hard study. You will also pass on gifts of good language to your family.

There is no substitute for regular practice of good language in developing skill as a communicator. Imitation through listening and reading out loud are two of the most powerful ways to do this, and they're easy to build into your everyday life.

Exercise. Pick up a newspaper and read something funny out loud in a way that a child would find interesting.

Exercise. Pick up a letter from your desk and read it out loud, using a tone that reflects the writer's personality.

Best Ways to Improve Your Vocabulary

If you travel often to other countries, you've probably been surprised at how quickly you've been able to learn enough foreign words to get by in daily activities. Maybe you've also been impressed with how readily new speakers of English have picked up the basics needed on a day-to-day basis.

The explanation is the same for both cases: **People need very few words for daily life.** Some people go through their entire lives with only a few hundred words. And everyone has a much smaller active vocabulary than they think they do.

Turn to any large dictionary and notice how many words you don't know. Webster's New International Dictionary contains hundreds of words starting with the letter **X**. Stop now and see if you can think of even one, or two or three.

Most people find unknown words every day in the media, books, and other people's conversation.

And yet, one strength of the truly remarkable communicator is possession of a large vocabulary. Every word you add to your vocabulary gives you power—the power to choose exactly the right word to express subtle shades of meaning and refined ideas.

One of the best ways to enlarge your vocabulary is read widely from good sources of material. In today's busy world, reading time is often limited. Most people read a lot every day for their jobs, or to keep up on important news, but you can learn a lot from choosing other types of material to build your vocabulary.

Look for well-written sources that write for an education audience. For leisure reading, choose pieces that are regarded as classics in any genre. Their use of language and vocabulary are powerful sources of improving your own word base.

Synonyms are words that can be used in place of other words with generally the same meaning. Knowing a wide variety of synonyms can add immeasurably to the richness and refinement of your speech. When someone asks if you enjoyed your meal at a trendy new restaurant, will you say,

> *"It was delicious!"*

Or will you say,

> *"It was spicy, with a light fruity sauce!"*

How much richer in meaning is the second sentence?

So study language. Keep a dictionary handy and take time to look up new words. Use a thesaurus when you write to find synonyms for expressions you use frequently. Use your new words in speech and writing. Resolve to pay attention to new words and learn as many of them as you can.

Make a habit of speaking with a full and rich vocabulary. Look for the exact right words that express the nuances of your thought. This practice will add greatly to your power and influence as a communicator.

Exercise. Look at the first page of words beginning with "a" in your dictionary. How many do you know? Write down three new ones and memorize them.

How to Use a Personal Slogan

During the European Middle Ages, it was common for knights to inscribe mottoes or family slogans on their shields. One famous motto was "Esperance en Dieu," or Hope in God—the motto of the English House of Percy.

These mottoes served two specific purposes which have

lessons for today. First, they increased the reputation of the knights, causing others to readily associate the knights with some lofty ideal.

They also influenced the men who used them to actually live up to those ideals.

The world of commerce and communication in modern times naturally uses lots of slogans and mottoes. Developing a powerful, memorable phrase to attach to one's product or service is a tried-and-true marketing tactic and one that has become a regular part of daily life.

Just like the knights of medieval times, individuals can make use of a personal slogan in their business lives. A carefully chosen personal slogan will have a positive effect on the person who uses it, and the people who hear it.

Let's look at some examples.

A young woman from a lower-class family has a personal slogan of "I do everything I set out to do." The result is an ever-growing determination that has led her to turn many failures into successes. She might see her dreams thwarted for years at a time, but time will show that in the end, she will succeed in nearly everything she sets out to do.

A highly respected businessman has the personal slogan, "I believe in being careful." This guiding principle has led him to become a master of finance, and a respected adviser on money management.

Think about your personal values—the ones that already guide you in your personal and business life. Which ideals are the ones that mean the most to you, about which you feel so strongly that you might even die to defend them if called on to do so? Every person holds many values at the same time, but most people can, if they sincerely examine themselves, identify one or two that are more important than any other.

Such a value can become the basis for a personal slogan that you can use to advantage in your business life. For example:

> *"I keep every promise I make."*
> *"People are more important to me than profits."*

> *"You can rely on me."*

Once you've figured out a personal slogan that genuinely fits your personality and values, try finding ways to work it into your business communications. Say it to yourself and others, and make a commitment to live up to it at all times.

You'll find that this simple tool can help you feel stronger personally and be more successful in your long-term communications with others.

Exercise. Think of some famous people who have phrases associated with their personalities. What is the value of each slogan, and do the famous individuals live up to them?

How to Use Questions to Influence Others

The hero in an old English novel achieved success in an unusual way. His name was Denry. Lacking wealth and a stellar education, he found a way to improve his lot in life significantly through artful speech.

One of the ways Denry did this was to ask questions. Little by little he acquired a reputation for wisdom and competence, without actually having a lot of either.

The story teaches a good lesson. Human beings naturally tend to avoid the "burden" of a conversation—that is, being put in a position that exposes us or makes us vulnerable.

Denry intuitively realized this. He knew that it was unwise to contradict others directly, because this put the burden of the conversation on the one doing the contradicting. However, it's easy to ask questions. The hero of the story did not respond to contradiction and he didn't answer questions. Instead, he put the full burden upon people he talked with by constantly asking questions like:

> *"Do you think so?"*
> *"What do you think?"*
> *"Is that your opinion?"*

Many people find this kind of conversation irresistible. People love to be asked their opinions and given the opportunity to say what they think. Those being asked

feel they are in a powerful position, and they might actually be. But the person asking the questions is really in the most powerful spot of all.

This method has the advantage of being entirely non-committal for the speaker, and draws out the full thoughts of others.

So try never to contradict or argue. Instead, give your companion the opportunity to assume the full burden of the conversation. Even though you seem to be yielding power, in fact you can gain an extraordinary amount of influence in the interchange.

There are times when it would be rude or offensive to express your opinion immediately. Be wholly non-committal, and allow the other person full sway.

Sometimes people you're with speak too quickly or hastily, not thinking through their ideas. You don't want to contradict them openly. However, you can say, "Do you think so?" and give others a chance to reconsider their opinions.

This method is very helpful in problematic situations. You can use it when you want to gain a temporary advantage or to "buy time." You can use it to show the weakness of someone else's argument. You can also benefit from this device when speaking with an angry or quarrelsome person.

Exercise. You have certain political views. A friend, who has opposite views, questions you and shows signs of starting to argue. How will you speak to avoid a conflict with your friend?

How to Prove a Point Using Inductive Logic

Inductive speech is a logical way of building a case when your audience might not be willing at first to accept your conclusions.

You can use this method in speaking and in constructing a piece of persuasive writing. Focus on learning how the logical progression works, and you can adapt it for a variety of communication needs.

In the beginning, in true induction, we don't actually know what our conclusions will be. For example, a salesman arranges his products in a certain way, more or less by accident. It happens that his sales go up, but he's not sure exactly why. When arranging his products in a certain way is followed many times with increased sales, he eventually concludes that the way he's arranging his goods is increasing sales.

Induction is a development from many details to a conclusion. It is, in general, the result of experimentation. It starts with a specific principle and builds to a general conclusion from them.

People who follow an inductive course of thought make their own experiments, make their own observations, and come to their own conclusions. They accept nothing on hearsay. Everything is the result of their own observation and thinking. They therefore come to their conclusions slowly, but once there, they'll tend to hang on to them firmly.

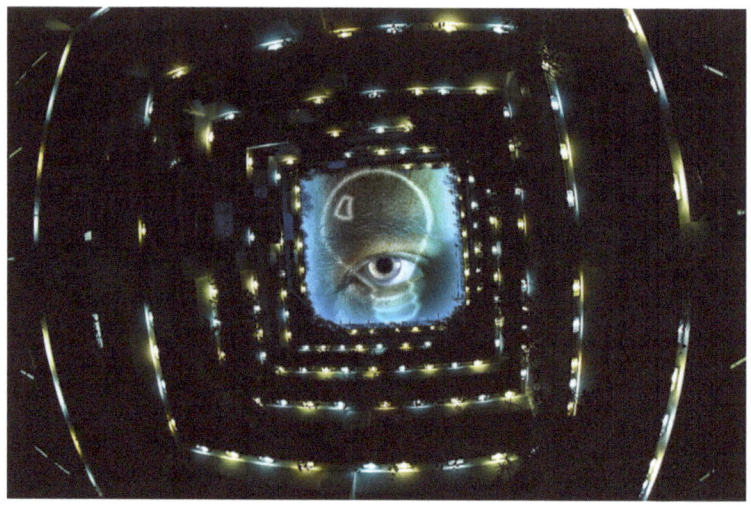

The president of a large company gave his salespeople complete outfits showing the raw materials used to make the company's products. He told the salespeople to demonstrate the steps of manufacture to potential buyers, and to explain that the materials were the best available, and that the manufacturing process was well thought-out.

The method worked. Potential buyers put the facts together, acknowledged that the products were extremely high quality, and placed orders.

You can use inductive reasoning in writing or verbal communications to persuade your audience of a desired conclusion.

How does it work?

First, call your audience's attention to some fact that they will readily admit or agree to. Proceed to a second fact, and then a third. Continue this way, every fact being one that will help the audience reach your conclusion in their own minds. Do not state the conclusion first. Let the audience observe and listen until the irrefutable conclusion "hits" them. Coming to it themselves will have much greater impact than if you simply state it yourself.

Exercise. Think of some specific item or service that you want to sell. Develop a set of inductive steps that will lead a potential client to make a purchase.

How to Prove a Point Using Deductive Logic

Like inductive logic, deductive reasoning can be used successfully in almost any situation in which you need to build an argument or a sales pitch. But, whereas inductive reasoning starts with a specific idea and builds to a general conclusion, deductive reasoning works the other way.

This kind of logic is at work in the world all around us, even if we don't recognize it as such. Studying how it works can help you build a thinking technique that can help you in persuasive communication, both in writing and in speaking.

In deductive reasoning, one goes from a known principle or conclusion to recognizing that a certain fact falls under the same principle or conclusion.

For example, most famous detective stories are based on deduction. The detective knows, for example, that a certain kind of manual work produces calluses on the hands. He sees a man whose hands have this type of callus. He concludes, therefore, that the stranger works in that particular field of labor.

There are three steps in this reasoning.

- Major Premise: Window washers have a certain pattern of calluses on their hands.
- Minor Premise: This stranger has that type of calluses.
- Conclusion: This stranger works as a window washer.

In deduction, if the major premise is true, and the minor premise is also true and related correctly to the major premise, the conclusion is irresistible.

In Edgar Allan Poe's classic detective story, "The Purloined Letter," a brilliant investigator must recover a letter from a cunning criminal.

The investigator uses deductive reasoning like this:

- An ordinary criminal would hide the letter in a very secret location.
- This criminal is not ordinary.
- Therefore he will not hide the letter in a secret place.
- Instead, he'll hide it where no one will look for it.
- He'll hide it in plain view where no one would suspect it.
- Therefore, the letter is somewhere in plain view.

The investigator visited the criminal's house and found the letter in plain sight, as he'd deduced he would.

Deductive reasoning can be very effective if the premises are strong. But it's possible, of course, to build an argument on bad logic. Many marketing messages that aim to use deduction start off with major premises that aren't really true.

Look at the following message outlined by a jewelry company for a campaign aimed at married men. What's wrong with the premises?

- Husbands should buy Valentine's Day gifts for their wives.
- Diamond jewelry makes a lovely gift.
- Your wife will love a diamond necklace for Valentine's Day.

In this case, there are probably holes in both premises. This argument might work for some audiences that generally agree that husbands should buy their wives gifts. But what if one's wife prefers pearls?

If you're going to use deductive reasoning to build a sales pitch or any other type of persuasive argument, think carefully about your premises. Often you will have the conclusion you want to reach already in mind. Since deduction tends to rely on absolutes, you'll need to consider what principles your audience is likely to agree on as generally accepted before you lay them out.

To sum up, when using deductive reasoning, state the principle first, and then prove that a specific fact falls within that principle.

Exercise. Develop a political nomination speech relying on deductive steps to show that your candidate should be elected.

Afterword

Congratulations!

If you've made it to the end of this book, you've studied many ideas and techniques for improving your communication. Hopefully you have also practiced enough of them to see a real difference in the way you interact with others.

You've been exposed to the foundations of good communication that men and women have used throughout history. You've also learned techniques for mastering business communications, public speaking, and being comfortable in social settings.

The lessons in this book are your tools. Keep reading and studying them, practicing as many as you can as you go about your professional and personal life. By continuing to do this, you will not fail to see a great improvement in all the ways you communicate.

These skills will help you speak and write more effectively—even with people who seem to have little in common with you.

They'll help set your mind at ease in situations where you might normally be nervous, because now you have guidelines that can be applied to almost any circumstance.

They'll also support you in becoming not only a good communicator, but one who leads by example.

At the end of the day, these tools will help you connect with other people so your interactions are more meaningful and rewarding. And after all, isn't that what communication is all about?

It's my hope that by using these ideas, you can experience more success, personal power, and happiness in your life and relationships.

Until next time,

Bill C.

Thank you so much for reading my book. I hope you really liked it.

As you probably know, many people look at the reviews on Amazon before they decide to purchase a book.

If you liked the book, could you please take a minute to leave a review with your feedback?

You can do that right here.
http://www.amazon.com/Shut-And-Talk-Bill-Calhoun/dp/9810770375

60 seconds is all I'm asking for, and it would mean the world to me.

Thank you so much,
Bill C.

More Books by Bill Calhoun:

Can't...Can!: How You CAN Get Motivated In Minutes

Good fortune is RARELY a result of chance. What we call

good luck is most often the result of planning, patience, perseverance and determination. Don't let "luck" take the credit for your hard work! I will tell you how to make your own good fortune in my book, "Can't?...CAN!" This is not a "rule book" that you have to follow word for word. Instead, it is a map that offers several guide-posts, side-roads, overpasses and bridges -- all heading toward self-fulfillment.

The suggestions in this book can help you find a real-time solution to your challenges and help you see alternatives that you may not have been aware of. I want to help you develop a structured path towards self-fulfillment, a path toward YOUR OWN brilliant lifestyle. Together, we are going to **create a Brand New YOU!**

No More Alps: A Survival Guide for Families Struggling with Bipolar Disorder

Don't spend your life afraid to reach for your Big Dreams. Bipolar and other Mood Disorders can make you FEEL trapped in an unfulfilling life, but the keys to transformation are in your hands. Learn how to overcome negative thought patterns and build your self-confidence with your Willpower, Imagination, and Daily Affirmations. So many of us today live a life that is incomplete not because we don't have what it takes, but because we are restricted by our own self-limiting thought and actions. The building of self-confidence is not hard, but it does require some effort. There is no need for exerting yourself to extremes here... simply read the material, absorb it and then... make it happen.

The Complete Guide For Kids' Nutrition: Fun & Healthy Eating For Children

Modern parents owe it to their children to guide their families' diets towards better food choices, better eating habits, and better health. This book contains tips and information to help your child establish healthy eating patterns and to help you make informed and positive choices for them. Together, you and your kids can lay the groundwork for a lifetime of healthy nutritional habits.

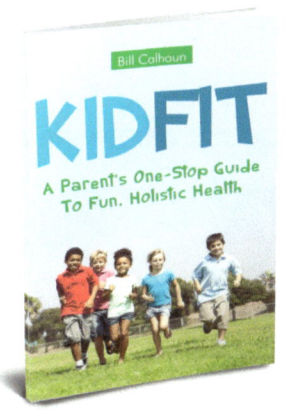

Kid Fit: A Parent's Fun, Holistic Guide To Healthy Kids

In light of the recently declared Obesity Epidemic, it is more important than ever before to start your kids off "on the right foot" by teaching them basic health habits early that will benefit them for a lifetime. This book covers the basics of why you should be concerned with and involved in your child's daily diet and activities and goes into specifics of how you can establish positive patterns and change negative ones. Active Kids are Fit Kids and Fit Kids are Healthy and Happy Kids!

Tiny EPIC Adventures for the Young at Heart

Original animal fables are brought to life in this beautifully illustrated series for the young and young at heart. Life lessons such as Belonging, Humility, Togetherness, and Courage are imparted through the whimsical adventures of animal protagonists.

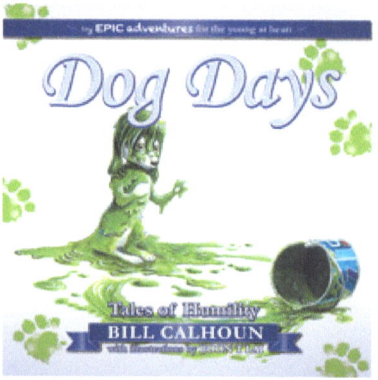

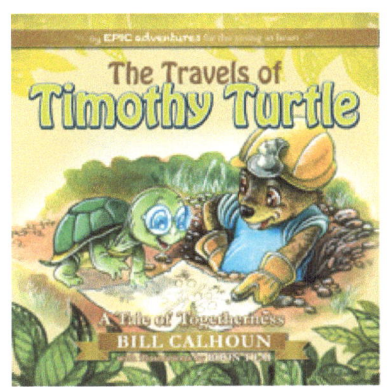

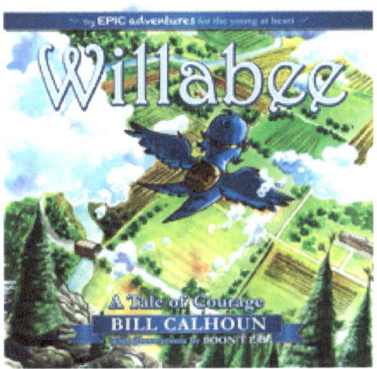

www.ingramcontent.com/pod-product-compliance
Lightning Source LLC
Chambersburg PA
CBHW041622220426
43662CB00001B/14